Astronomers

BY ROBERTA SILMAN

Table of Contents

Early Astronomers

Astronomers are people who study the sun, moon, stars, planets, and other objects in the sky. The word "astronomer" comes from two Greek words: "*astro*," meaning "star," and "*nemein*," which means "arrange." In ancient Greece, astronomers were thought of as "those who arrange the stars."

An ancient Greek astronomer gazes at the stars.

The ancient Greek astronomers believed that the sun traveled around Earth. This seemed to make perfect sense considering that they could see the sun moving across the sky and could not feel Earth moving.

SEE THE SUN "MOVE" FOR YOURSELF!

On the next clear day, go out early in the morning and locate the sun in the sky. The easiest way to do this is to site it above a tree or a building. Then, go out a few hours later and locate the sun again. Is it over the same tree or building? In fact, if you mark the location of the sun every hour during the day, you'll see that it will appear to move slowly westward across the sky. But the sun is not really moving. The Earth is.

This photo was made by taking pictures of the sun at different times of the day on the same piece of film. It shows how the sun seems to move across the sky.

When the early Greek astronomers looked at the stars, they noticed that some of them made patterns. The astronomers called these patterns **constellations** (kahn-steh-LAY-shunz). They also noticed that although these constellations moved around in the sky, the patterns they made always looked the same.

There was one problem, however. Of all the stars that the astronomers saw in the sky, there were five bright stars that did not stay in patterns. Instead, these five seemed to wander back and forth across the constellations. Sometimes these "wandering stars" would even stop for a while and then appear to move backward. Not knowing what these strange objects were, the Greek astronomers simply called them planets, which is the Greek word for "wanderer"!

THE FIRST FIVE PLANETS

The telescope was not invented until the early 1600s. Before that time, astronomers believed that there were only five planets because that was all they could see without using magnification. The five planets they knew of were Mercury, Venus, Mars, Jupiter, and Saturn.

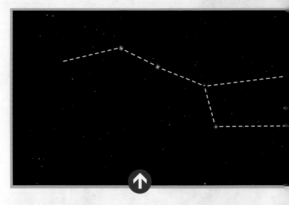

The Big Dipper is one of the easiest constellations to find in the sky.

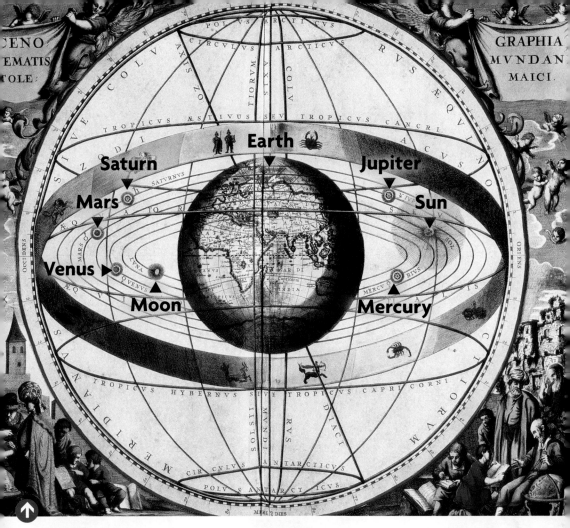

This drawing illustrates Ptolemy's view of how the sun, moon, and five planets circled Earth.

In about A.D. 140, the famous Greek astronomer Ptolemy (TAH-leh-mee) made a **model** of what he thought the **universe** looked like. Borrowing ideas from other astronomers, he put Earth at the center and everything else—the sun, moon, stars, and the five known planets—moving around Earth in perfect circles.

For more than 1,300 years, most people accepted this view of the universe. It was not until Nicolaus Copernicus finally questioned it in the 1500s that things began to change.

Nicolaus Copernicus

Nicolaus Copernicus
(1473–1543)

Poland

Although this drawing shows Nicolaus Copernicus looking through a telescope, that would not have been possible. The telescope was not invented until about 1608.

Nicolaus Copernicus was born in Poland in 1473. The son of a trader, Copernicus was raised by a rich uncle. His uncle encouraged him to go to schools in Poland and Italy to study law, art, mathematics, and medicine. At school, astronomy fascinated Copernicus. He began to spend a lot of time studying the planets and the ways in which they moved in the sky.

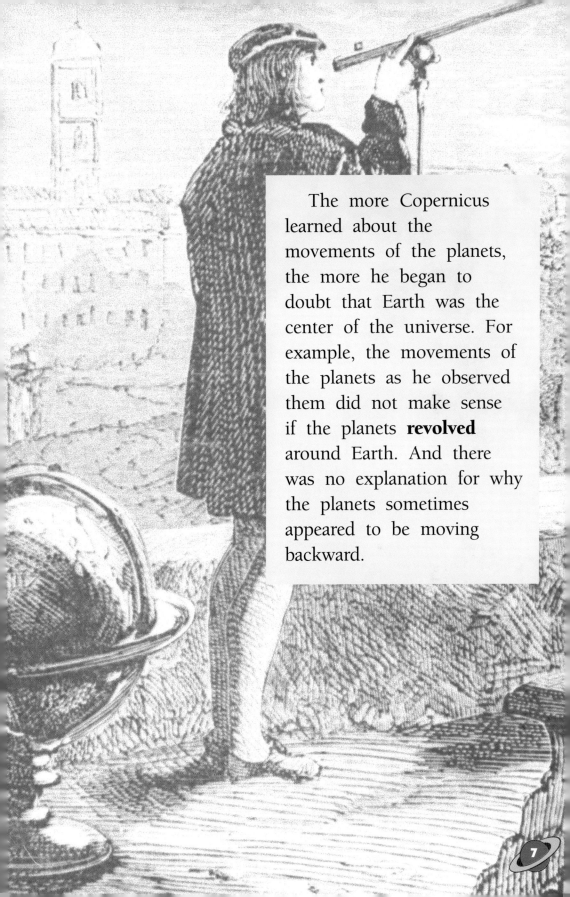

The more Copernicus learned about the movements of the planets, the more he began to doubt that Earth was the center of the universe. For example, the movements of the planets as he observed them did not make sense if the planets **revolved** around Earth. And there was no explanation for why the planets sometimes appeared to be moving backward.

Copernicus believed that Earth and the other planets revolved around the sun.

THINK IT OVER!

The next time you're driving in a car on the highway, you can see what Copernicus meant when he observed that the planets sometimes seemed to be moving backward. Ask the person who is driving to pull alongside a car and match its speed for a few seconds. Then, ask your driver to slowly pass that car. From where you are sitting, the other car will look as if it is moving backward!

While reading books about the ancient Greeks, Copernicus learned that in 260 B.C. someone had suggested that Earth revolved around the sun. Although no one had believed it at the time, Copernicus became curious about this possibility. He began to look for **data** to support it.

Copernicus discovered that the movements of the planets made sense if the planets were revolving around the sun rather than around Earth. He also realized that this would explain why the planets sometimes seemed to be moving backward in the sky. The planets were not actually moving backward; Earth was just passing them as it, too, revolved around the sun.

Now Copernicus was sure that the sun was the center of the universe. In 1515, he started working on a book to explain his ideas.

At that time, however, most people were not open to the idea that the planets revolved around the sun. They liked the idea that Earth was the center of the universe. It made them feel special. Powerful religious leaders had even gone so far as to make the idea part of church law. And, at the time, anyone who disobeyed church law could be put to death! Wisely, Copernicus planned to share his ideas only with his closest friends.

WATCH WHAT YOU SAY!

People who disagreed with the religious leaders were called heretics. Often, they were put on trial and, if they did not change their beliefs, they were tortured, thrown in jail, and even burned at the stake!

In 1530, however, some religious leaders found out about Copernicus's book. When they questioned him about it, he explained that he was simply wondering about things, not stating facts. He assured them that he was not disagreeing with church law, so they let him go.

Over the next twelve years, Copernicus wrote another book that explained his ideas in greater detail. Again, he did not plan to publish it, but a friend persuaded him to.

In May 1543, Copernicus's book was published. Unfortunately, this great astronomer never got the chance to defend his work. He died soon after the book was published.

It would be left up to another man, by the name of Galileo Galilei, to defend Copernicus's work.

Giordano Bruno (1548–1600), an Italian philosopher, was burned at the stake in 1600 because he openly stated that the sun was the center of the universe.

REVOLVTIONVM LIB. I. 2ĩ

30 **anno** fuum complet circuitum. Poft hunc Iupiter duodecennali revolutione mobilis. Deinde Mars , qui biennio circuit. Quartum in ordine annua revolutio locum obtinet , in quo terram cum orbe

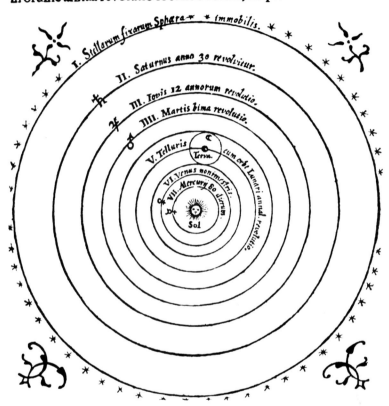

Iunari tanquam epicyclo contineri diximus. Quinto loco Venus nono menfe reducitur. Sextum denique locum Mercurius tenet , octuaginta dierum fpacio circumcurrens. In medio vero omnium refidet Sol. Quis enim in hoc pulcherrimo templo lampadem hanc in alio vel meliori loco poneret , quam unde totum fimul poffit illuminare? Siquidem non inepte quidam lucernam mundi, alij mentem , alij rectorem vocant.Trimefgiftus *vifibilem Deum,*Sophoclis Electra *intuentem omnia.* Ita profecto tanquam in folio regali Sol refidens

Solis nom Rẽg feu attributæ

F 5020.

C 3

This page from a book by Copernicus illustrates his view of the solar system.

Galileo Galilei

This painting shows Galileo observing how a chandelier swings back and forth.

Italy

Galileo Galilei (1564–1642)

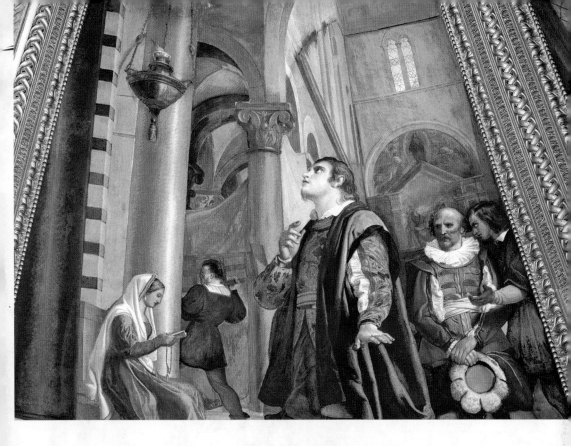

Galileo Galilei, often known only by his first name, was born in Italy in 1564, twenty-one years after Copernicus died. Galileo's father was a merchant and a musician. He sent Galileo to school to study medicine, but Galileo soon became interested in science and mathematics.

Galileo made his first important discovery in 1583 when he was only nineteen years old. Sitting in a church, Galileo watched a chandelier swing back and forth. He used his **pulse** to time the swings of the chandelier. Soon he began to notice something important. Regardless of whether the chandelier took a very long swing or a very short swing, it always took the same number of heartbeats for it to return to its starting point.

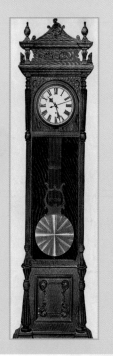

Galileo called the chandelier a **pendulum**. He suggested that the regular swing of a pendulum could be used to measure time. His idea later led to the invention of the first reliable clock.

Galileo was good at mathematics and was soon offered a job teaching it. As a teacher, he soon became famous for doing **experiments**.

Here is a drawing of
the clock invented
by Galileo.

Although there is no
record of it, it is said that
Galileo's most famous
experiment involved
dropping balls from the
Leaning Tower of Pisa,
in Italy. For about 2,000
years, people had been
taught to believe that if
a heavy object and a
light object were dropped
at the same time, the
heavier one would always
hit the ground first.
Legend has it that Galileo
stood at the top of the
Leaning Tower of Pisa and
dropped a light wooden
ball and a heavy iron ball
at the same time. Much to
everyone's surprise, the
two balls hit the ground
at the same time!

'They were seen to fall evenly.'

In this drawing, a crowd gathers
to watch Galileo perform his
famous experiment from the
Leaning Tower of Pisa.

In 1609, Galileo learned of a new invention, a simple telescope that allowed people to see distant objects close up. Galileo built his own telescope so that he could get a closer look at the stars and planets. Galileo's telescope magnified things about thirty times, making it possible to see things never before seen.

Q. Galileo observed Neptune through his telescope but thought it was just a star!

Many people were interested in seeing the stars through a telescope. This drawing shows Galileo demonstrating his telescope in Italy.

mountains

craters ▶

When you look through binoculars at a full moon, you can see craters, seas, and other features.

Galileo discovered many things when he looked through his telescope. When he looked at the moon, he saw **craters** and mountains.

See What Galileo Saw!

You can see what Galileo saw. All you need is a pair of binoculars. Start by looking at the full moon. Can you locate any of the craters? Those big dark patches are what Galileo called seas. Although these seas have no water in them, they were once filled with lava!

If you're really up for a challenge, try to spot any of Jupiter's moons. They will look like little white dots that move back and forth on either side of the planet.

Galileo also observed that Jupiter had four moons that circled the planet, not Earth. In addition, he noticed things about Venus that convinced him it was moving around the sun, not around Earth.

THE MOONS OF JUPITER

Today, we know that Jupiter has at least forty-nine moons. The four moons that Galileo discovered are named Callisto, Europa, Ganymede, and Io. All four are often called the Galilean moons in his honor. Ganymede is Jupiter's largest moon. It is bigger than the planet Mercury!

Galileo wrote about his observations of the sky in this notebook.

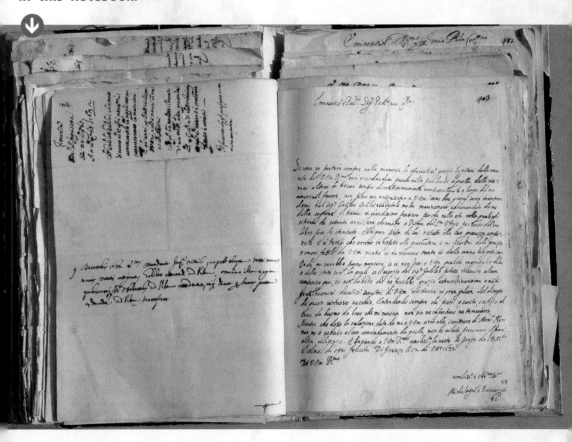

Like Copernicus before him, Galileo was now certain that the sun was the center of the universe.

In 1610, Galileo published a book that outlined his discoveries. Then he traveled to Rome to discuss his findings with religious leaders. Galileo wanted them to know that Copernicus had been right. But the religious leaders were not pleased with Galileo. They still wanted to believe that Earth was the center of the universe.

Galileo began to say more and more openly that Copernicus had been right. When he published another book in 1629, the religious leaders arrested him and put him on trial. They threatened to torture him and then finally sentenced him to life in prison.

By this time, Galileo was seventy years old and almost blind. Instead of jailing Galileo, the religious leaders decided that he should spend the rest of his life locked up in his own house. Although he lived for nine more years, he was never able to teach again. Galileo died in 1642 at the age of seventy-eight.

This portrait shows Galileo near the end of his life.

Galileo stands before the religious leaders.

IT'S A
FACT!

It took years for the religious leaders to accept the fact that Galileo had been right. Even when they did, the charges against Galileo were not dropped. It was not until 1992 that Pope John Paul II finally cleared Galileo's name—350 years after his death!

Johannes Kepler

← Johannes Kepler
(1571–1630)

↑

Germany

Johannes (yoh-HAHN-es) Kepler was born in Germany in 1571, seven years after Galileo's birth. The son of a poor soldier, Kepler did not have an easy childhood. At the age of five, he got smallpox, a serious disease that left him with crippled hands and bad eyesight.

Like Copernicus, Kepler at first ➡ believed that the planets moved around the sun in perfect circles.

Kepler was very smart, however. He went to school planning to study **philosophy** and religion. At school, he learned about Copernicus and became interested in astronomy and mathematics. Like Galileo, he did so well in these subjects that he went on to teach them himself.

By this time, most astronomers believed that the sun was the center of the universe. But they also mistakenly believed that the planets revolved around the sun in paths shaped like perfect circles. Even Kepler thought this was true. Because of this belief, however, the motions of the planets as seen from Earth could not be explained.

SPOTLIGHT ON TYCHO BRAHE

BORN:

December 14, 1546, in Sweden

OCCUPATION:

Astronomer to European kings

ACHIEVEMENT:

Charted the positions of stars and planets accurately for the first time

INTERESTING FACT:

In a duel with his cousin over who was the better mathematician, Brahe had his nose sliced off. From that day on, Brahe had to wear a fake nose that was made out of gold and held on with wax!

DIED:

October 24, 1601

For eight long years, Kepler studied data collected by another brilliant astronomer, Tycho Brahe (TEE-koh BRAH), with whom he had worked. Finally, in 1609 (the same year in which Galileo turned his telescope to the sky), Kepler came up with a mathematical **formula** that explained the true motion of the planets. This formula proved that the planets revolved around the sun in oval paths, not in circles. This oval shape is called an **ellipse**.

Our understanding of the solar system is based in part on Kepler's formulas. Today we know that the planets travel in ellipses around the sun, not in circles.

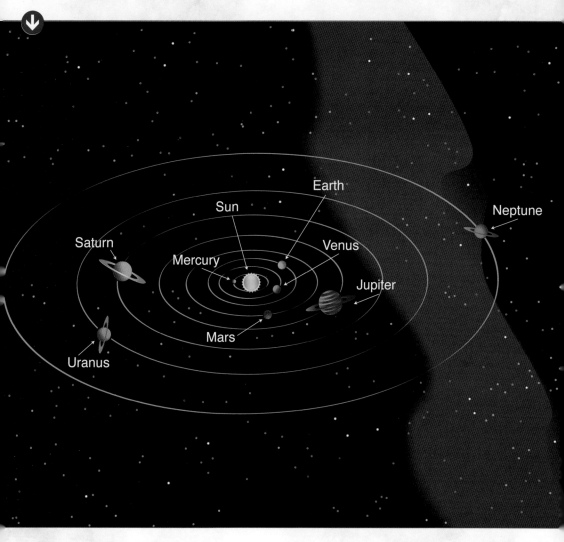

Sun

Earth

Neptune

Saturn

Mercury

Venus

Jupiter

Mars

Uranus

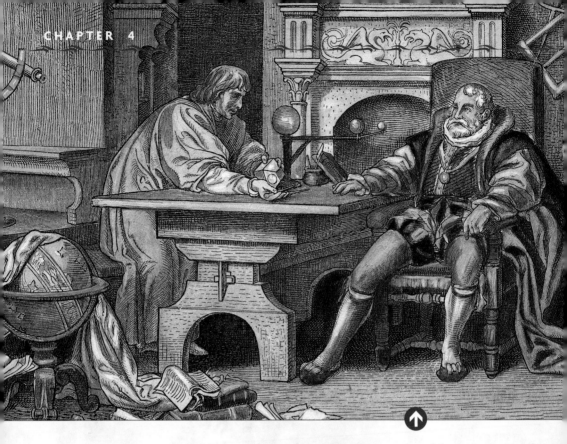

In 1609, Kepler published a book that presented all of his findings. In it, he also described some rules that explained the motions of the planets. These rules proved that Copernicus had been right and that the sun was the center of the universe. Using mathematics and **logic**, Kepler had solved one of the great puzzles of modern science.

When Kepler died in 1630 at the age of fifty-nine, he knew that he had helped to change astronomy forever. Today, many people consider him the father of modern astronomy.

In this painting, Johannes Kepler shows Emperor Rudolph II how the planets travel around the sun.

Astronomers: Past, Present, and Future

People have always looked up at the sky and tried to make sense out of what they saw. They used mathematics as a tool and made models to help them understand what was happening. Sometimes, the models were wrong, and it took people such as Copernicus, Galileo, and Kepler to set the record straight.

While Copernicus may have started the revolution in astronomy, it did not end with Kepler. Other scientists built upon the work of these great astronomers and made their own contributions.

The history books are filled with stories of great men and women who spent countless hours studying the night sky, adding to what was already known.

Turn the page to meet some of these famous astronomers.

Maria Mitchell ➡

(1818–1889),
an American astronomer,
discovered a comet in 1847
and became the first
woman elected to the
American Academy of Arts
and Sciences.

⬅ Annie Jump Cannon

(1863–1941),
an American astronomer,
worked at the Harvard
College Observatory and
developed a huge catalog
of objects in space. While
examining photos, she
discovered five novas and
almost 300 stars. Cannon
was the first woman to
receive an honorary
doctoral degree from the
University of Oxford.

Edwin Hubble →
(1889–1953),

an American astronomer, took astronomy outside our galaxy. He was responsible for discovering new galaxies and calculating how far those galaxies were from our own.

← Carl Sagan
(1934–1996),

an American astronomer, wrote many books and created television shows that helped people better understand outer space. He worked closely with the National Aeronautics and Space Administration and helped with many space missions. Sagan was the first scientist to prove that Mars was a cold planet and Venus was hot.

As you have seen, Copernicus, Galileo, Kepler, and many other early astronomers helped humans understand our world in a new way.

Today's astronomers are pushing the boundaries of exploration even farther. Using powerful new tools and deeper mathematical understandings, they are mapping distant stars, moons, and planets that early astronomers could only have imagined.

The more astronomers learn about the universe, the more questions they raise. And as future astronomers look to the stars, there will doubtless be many new mysteries for them to solve.

Glossary

constellation   (kahn-steh-LAY-shun) a group of stars that forms a pattern

craters   (KRAY-terz) hollow areas

data   (DAY-tuh) pieces of information

ellipse   (ih-LIPS) a shape that looks like a narrow or flattened circle

experiments   (ik-SPAIR-ih-ments) tests that are used to prove something

formula   (FOR-myuh-luh) a rule

logic   (LAH-jik) reasoning

model   (MAH-dul) an example of something

pendulum   (PEN-juh-lum) a weight that is hung from a fixed point in such a way that it swings back and forth

philosophy   (fih-LAH-suh-fee) the study of beliefs about life

pulse   (PULS) the beat of the arteries, which is caused by the pumping of the heart

revolved   (rih-VAHLVD) moved around an object in a fixed path

universe   (YOO-nih-vers) everything that exists, including Earth, the other planets, stars, and all of space

Index

Write in Your Science Journal

Choose one of the following prompts to write about in your journal. Make drawings, charts, or other graphic features to help you organize your thoughts.

1. Write about something in space that interests you. It could be a planet, star, or galaxy. Make a list of questions you would like to answer about it. (Make connections)

2. Review the text. Explain how the work of Galileo and Kepler expanded on the ideas of Copernicus. (Summarize information)

3. The author included dramatic details of how the work of these three astronomers was rejected by people at that time. Why do you think this was so? What does it tell you about the way in which people sometimes react to new ideas? (Make judgments)

...dits
...or: Alison Adams
...igner: Christine Kilavos
...to Researcher: Colleen Fleischhauer
...racy Consultants: Frances Fincher and May Tilghman,
...Vake County Public School System, Raleigh, North Carolina
...tent Reviewer: Steve Tomecek

...to Credits
...er, Page 23: Dennis Diciccio/Corbis; Page 5: Mike Zens/Corbis; Pages 8, 10, 12, 15,
...19, 28: Roger Ressmeyer/Corbis; Pages 9, 14, 21, 26: Corbis; Page 11: Photo Library
...rnational/Corbis; Page 13A: Reuters NewMedia Inc./Corbis; Page 24: Bettmann/
...bis; Page 25: Agence France Presse/Corbis; Page 29: Jonathan Blain/Corbis; Page 30:
...rence Manning/Corbis;
...s by Mike Hortens
...rations by Albert Hanner

NAVIGATORS

BENCHMARK EDUCATION COMPANY
629 Fifth Avenue • Pelham, NY • 10803

Astronomers

Today we take for granted the fact that Earth, like all the other planets, orbits the sun. Long ago, however, most people believed that Earth was the center of the solar system. Meet three brilliant, determined early astronomers who used their observations and mathematical understandings to prove Earth's true position in relation to the sun.

ABOUT THE AUTHOR

Roberta Silman is the author of *Somebody Else's Child*, a book for children, and stories and novels for adults (*Blood Relations*, *Boundaries*, *The Dream Dredger*, and *Beginning the World Again*). Originally a science writer, she has always been interested in astronomy.

ISBN 978-1-4509-0684-5

9 781450 906845

BENCHMARK EDUCATION COMPANY